Disclaimer

This book is provided "as-is" and expresses the author's views and opinions. The views, opinions and information expressed in this book, including URL and other Internet website references, may change without notice.

Source Files

The source files for this guide, including all PowerShell scripts, the Excel workbook and ODC connection files, can be downloaded at http://1drv.ms/1Qaf31g

Requirements

This guide assumes you are familiar with administering Microsoft System Center Configuration Manager, and running PowerShell scripts. The guide is designed around Configuration Manager 2012 R2 and PowerShell 4.0, but scripts that run on client machines are compatible with PowerShell 2.0.

About the Author

Trevor Jones works as a Senior Windows Systems Administrator for a global semiconductor company. He has 10 years IT experience and works frequently with Microsoft System Center Configuration Manager and PowerShell. He is an active blogger at http://smsagent.wordpress.com.

Contents

Introduction

Java, or the Java Runtime Environment, is one of those applications that many Windows computers worldwide have installed. According to the Java website *"97% of Enterprise Desktops Run Java"* and *"89% of Desktops (or Computers) in the U.S. Run Java"*[1]. If such figures can be believed, then deploying, updating and managing Java in an enterprise environment is of certain interest to IT administrators. Given the security concerns associated with Java and the frequency of new Java releases, IT administrators need to have a robust solution that allows new versions of Java to be deployed in a timely manner, control which version/s of Java are installed in your environment, and allows you to control the configuration of Java across all your machines.

The purpose of this document is to demonstrate how Microsoft System Center Configuration Manager can be used to accomplish this. A 3rd-party patching solution for Configuration Manager can help with the deployment and updating of Java, however it is possible to build an efficient and reliable solution using native Configuration Manager capability, together with PowerShell. Each organization will have their own requirements for Java, but this guide presents a detailed, step-by-step demonstration of how Configuration Manager can be used to:

1. Deploy Java Runtime, 32-bit by default and 64-bit where required
2. Ensure that *only* the version you are deploying is installed, and remains installed across all your machines (exceptions permitted)
3. Ensure that Java is configured according to the security settings required in your environment, across all machines
4. Update Java to a new version in an easy-to-use, automated process

As a bonus, we will also demonstrate a custom deployment report with Microsoft Excel that will allow easy, real-time monitoring of your Java deployments.

The solution presented in this guide does not represent the *only* way to deploy Java using Configuration Manager and PowerShell, but it does demonstrate the capability of both to meet the business requirement.

Overview

In this section, we will give a more detailed overview of what this solution achieves and how it does it.

Deploy Java

First we will create two Java Applications in Configuration Manager (ConfigMgr for short), one for 32-bit and one for 64-bit Java. By default, all our client machines will get the Java 32-bit installed, and the 64-bit version will be available upon request. Instead of using the Application Supersedence model to handle Java updates, we will create a new Deployment Type for each new Java version in the same Application. This is simpler and more effective as we do not need to create new Applications and retire old ones and, if we want to, we can use the same Application Deployments to roll out the new Java version. It also allows us to use a custom uninstall script to remove older versions of Java, which is often necessary because there may be many different versions of Java installed on our client machines, and we want to

---

[1] https://www.java.com/en/about/

be able to uninstall any of them. Additionally, it will allow us to perform some cleanup activities such as removing stale registry keys and environment variables that can be left behind by previous installations, which can prevent new installations from succeeding.

The Applications will be created with an internal dependency, ie the INSTALL deployment type is dependent on the UNINSTALL deployment type, which therefore must be evaluated first. For the UNINSTALL deployment type, we will use a custom detection method to determine if the currently deployed version is installed, and if it's not, the UNINSTALL script will run to remove any other Java versions that may be installed. When finished, the standard MSI code detection method of the INSTALL deployment type will be evaluated and ensure that the current version gets installed.

Using the ConfigMgr client's Application Deployment Evaluation cycle together with our custom detection script and our custom uninstall script allows us to create a kind of *compliance* scenario where we ensure that all machines have the same version of Java installed. When the Application Deployment Evaluation cycle runs on the client machine, which is every 7 days by default, the ConfigMgr client will re-evaluate the Java Application, running first the detection method of the UNINSTALL deployment type to determine if the currently deployed version is installed, and if there are any other Java versions that have been installed since the last cycle. If the machine is not compliant to the current version, the other version/s will be removed and the currently deployed version installed again.

Of course, there are always some clients that are exceptions and may require a particular version or even multiple versions of Java to be installed, for example for application compatibility, so for these machines we will create an exclusion collection and Java installations will be handled manually or through a separate Application deployment.

In this guide, we will target *devices* rather than *users* when deploying our Java application.

Control Java

Many enterprises will want to control how Java is configured on their client machines. For example, they want to lock down certain settings in the Java Control Panel, preventing users from making changes, or preventing Java from auto-updating, to set the security level, or to create a whitelist of allowed sites etc. Oracle provide some tools to help accomplish this, including the deployment.properties file and the Deployment Rule set. In this guide, we will use ConfigMgr Compliance settings to deploy a system-level deployment.properties file to all our clients, the content of which will be controlled by the IT administration team. Using Compliance settings allows us to keep control of how Java is configured on our clients. Where some users have administrative rights and may be able to change the Java configuration themselves, Compliance settings will ensure that those machines remain compliant by remediating any unwanted changes.

Update Java

Given the frequency of new Java releases, the increased risk of security exploits in older Java versions and the somewhat annoying 'Your Java version is out of date' prompt hard-coded into the Java RE, it's important to keep our client machines updated to the latest version. To update Java on our client machines we need to do the following:

1. Download and extract the new binaries
2. Create a new deployment type in the Java Application
3. Disable or remove the old deployment type
4. Distribute content files to distribution points

5. Update the detection method of the Uninstall script
6. Set a date for the deployment to begin

Instead of doing this manual work with every Java release, we will automate the entire process with PowerShell, making Java updates a breeze.

Deploy Java

Download Java Binaries

First, let's download the latest Java binaries. We will extract the exe file and use the MSI contained within it. From the source files, use the following PowerShell script to automate this:

Invoke-JavaBinaryDownload.ps1

By default it will download the latest 32-bit Java executable and save it to your %USERPROFILE%\Downloads directory, but you can also download the 64-bit Java executable using the – Architecture switch, and specify a different download location if desired, for example:

Invoke-JavaBinaryDownload.ps1 –Architecture 64-bit -DownloadLocation C:\temp

If you prefer to do it manually:

1. Browse to http://www.java.com/en/download/manual.jsp and download the **Windows Offline installer** for either 32 or 64-bit.
2. Double-click the executable file to begin the extraction, then cancel the installation window when it appears
3. Navigate to C:\users\%USERNAME%\AppData\LocalLow\Sun\Java

Copy the extracted directory to your ConfigMgr package source location, for example copy the **jre1.8.0_45** directory to \\<SCCMServer>\PackageSource\Java.

Create a 32-bit Java Application

In this section, we will create a ConfigMgr Application for the 32-bit Java Runtime. This is the default version of Java that will be deployed to all our client machines. We will also create later an Application for 64-bit Java, but this will not be deployed to all our machines, only when it is needed or requested by the end user. As we described in the Introduction, this is the only Application we will create for 32-bit Java as we will not use the Application Supersedence capability for updating Java, but instead simply create a new deployment type in the Application for each new version of Java we deploy. This gives us the following benefits:

1. We can use a single Application for all our 32-bit Java deployments, which eases administration and means we don't have to create a new Application, supersede the old one, then disable or delete it for each new Java version we deploy
2. We can use an existing deployment in the Application to target our computers. Once the new deployment type is created and the old one disabled or removed, the targeted computers will re-evaluate the deployment, determine that the Application is no longer installed because of the new MSI code, then install it from the new deployment type.
3. Content distribution will happen automatically once the new deployment type has been created
4. We can use a custom PowerShell script to ensure that all other versions of Java are removed cleanly, and that only the deployed Java version remains.

Because we will create a dependency between the INSTALL and the UNINSTALL deployment types, so that the UNINSTALL DT must be evaluated first, we can use a custom PowerShell detection method for the UNINSTALL DT to control whether the UNINSTALL DT actually needs to run. For example, if the detection method determines that ONLY the currently deployed version of Java is installed, then the

UNINSTALL script doesn't need to run. If however, it detects any other version of Java, it will go ahead and run the UNINSTALL script to remove it. This ensures that all our client machines have only the intended version of Java installed.

How the UNINSTALL PowerShell Script Works

When the UNINSTALL script runs on a client machine, it will do the following:

1. Check for any Java-related processes that may be running, and kill them, so they don't cause the uninstallation to fail.
2. Check for any open browsers and close them, in case Java is being used in the browser, so they don't cause the uninstallation to fail. The list of browsers that will be checked for is defined in the **$Browsers** variable at the beginning of the script. Customise this as you need.
3. The Uninstall branch in the 32-bit and 64-bit registry nodes (where applicable) will then be searched for ANY installed version of the Java Runtime, 32 or 64-bit, using certain keywords to exclude, for example, the Java Development kit.
4. Each version of Java will be uninstalled in turn using MSIEXEC and the product code
5. With some versions of Java, there is a known bug in the MSI that causes a pop-up during uninstallation, as described in this article: http://windowsexplored.com/2013/10/23/failed-java-uninstalls/. To handle that, the script will watch to see if the pop-up appears, then kill the process that hosts it, to allow the uninstallation to successfully complete.
6. The script will then check some known registry locations and environment variables that may have been left behind by the uninstaller and remove them, so they don't cause the installation of the new version to fail.
7. Finally, because the script will remove *even the currently deployed Java version*, in order to make sure that registry keys etc are clean, it will then trigger the Application Deployment Evaluation Cycle in the ConfigMgr client. This action causes the client to re-evaluate the Application deployments assigned to it, and in the case where the current version of Java has been removed, it will be immediately re-installed. This will also be true for the 64-bit Java version, if deployed to the machine. **To be sure that the current Java version is reinstalled, the client computer must remain in the collection targeted by the deployment.**

How the Detection Method Script for the UNINSTALL Deployment Type Works

The PowerShell script used for the detection method of the UNINSTALL deployment type works by searching the "HKLM:\SOFTWARE\JavaSoft\Java Runtime Environment" registry branch (and the "HKLM:\SOFTWARE\Wow6432Node\JavaSoft\Java Runtime Environment" for 64-bit OS) for any version of Java Runtime that is **not** the currently deployed version. The current version number is defined in the **$CurrentVersion** variable at the beginning of the script, and must be updated when a new version of Java is deployed.

If no other version of Java is installed, then we return "Compliant" to satisfy the detection and the UNINSTALL script does not run. If any other version of Java is installed, whether 32 or 64-bit, then we return no output to fail the detection and the UNINSTALL script will then run and remove the other Java versions.

The actual logic of the script can be seen in the following process flow diagram:

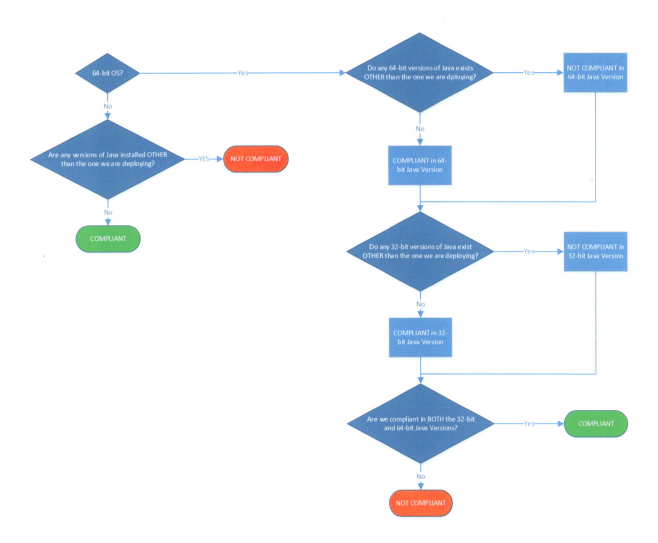

Create the Application

In the ConfigMgr console, navigate to the **Software Library > Applications** node and **click Create Application** in the ribbon.

In the **Create Application Wizard**, use the **Windows Installer** type and browse to the location of your Java MSI file in your package source.

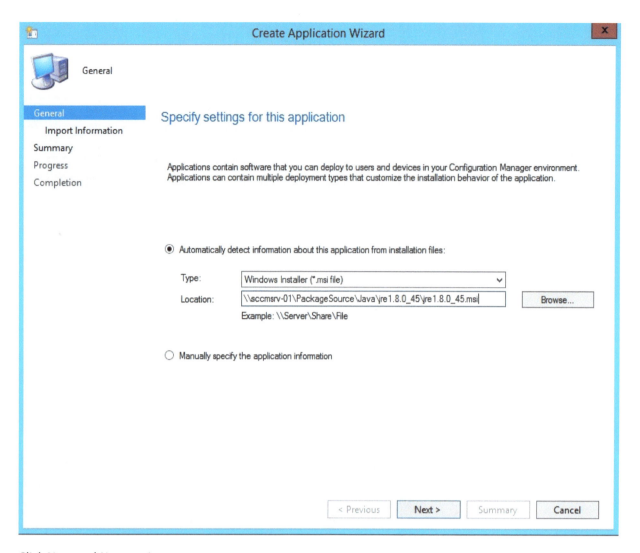

Click Next and Next again.

Name the Application **Java**. Since the application itself will never be superseded, we can use the same application for each new version of Java released and give it a more generic name.

Enter additional metadata, such as **Administrator comments** and **Publisher**.

To suppress any reboot, add the **REBOOT=ReallySuppress** switch to the installation program.

Install for system, and check the box '**Run installation program as 32-bit process**...'

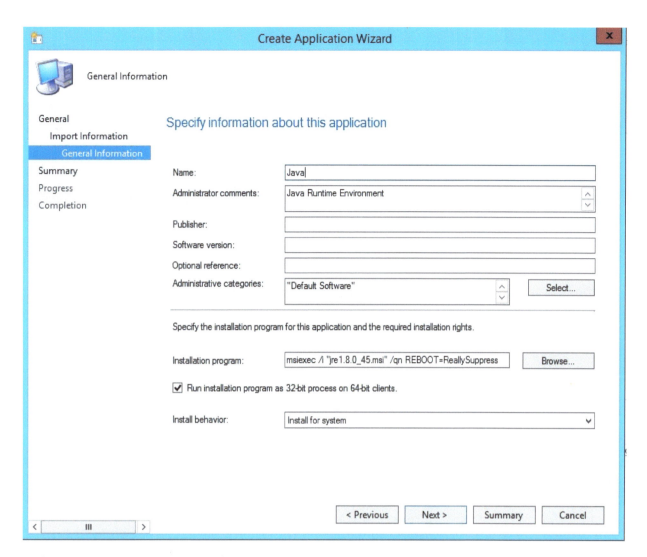

Click Next, Next again, and Close to finish.

In the ConfigMgr Console, click on the application and click the **Deployment Types** tab at the bottom.

Right-click the deployment type and choose **Properties**.

On the **General** tab, remove the " **– Windows Installer (*.msi file)**" from the Name:

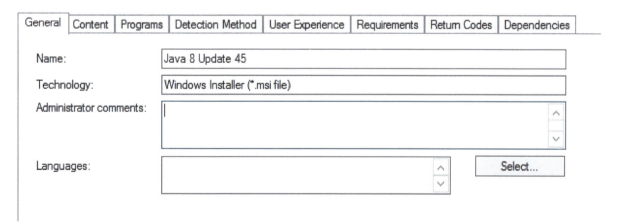

On the **Programs** tab, click Browse at the bottom and select the MSI file to add the **Product Code**:

General	Content	Programs	Detection Method	User Experience	Requirements	Return Codes	Dependencies

Specify the command to install this application.

Installation program: `msiexec /i jre1.8.0_45.msi /qn REBOOT=ReallySuppress` [Browse...]

Installation start in: [ ]

Specify the command to uninstall this application.

Uninstall program: `msiexec /x {26A24AE4-039D-4CA4-87B4-2F83218045F0} /q` [Browse...]

Uninstall start in: [ ]

☑ Run installation and uninstall program as 32-bit process on 64-bit clients.

Windows Source management enables an .msi represented by this Deployment Type to automatically be updated or repaired from content source files on an available distribution point. Specify the Windows Installer product code to enable installation source management.

Product code: `{26A24AE4-039D-4CA4-87B4-2F83218045F0}` [Browse...]

Click OK to save the changes.

Create an UNINSTALL Deployment Type

Now that we have the application object, let's add a deployment type that will uninstall other versions of Java.

From the source files, copy the PowerShell script **Invoke-JavaUninstallation.ps1** to a subfolder in your Package source, for example \\<Sccmserver>\PackageSource\Java\UninstallScript.

In the ribbon, click **Create Deployment Type**. In the **Create Deployment Type Wizard**, choose the **Script Installer** type, then click Next.

Enter the Name **Uninstall Java** and click Next.

In the **Content location**, browse to the folder that contains the PowerShell script. In the **Installation program**, enter the following:

powershell.exe -ExecutionPolicy Bypass -File .\Invoke-JavaUninstallation.ps1

Specify information about the content to be delivered to target devices

General
  General Information
  Content
  Detection Method
  User Experience
  Requirements
  Dependencies
Summary
Progress
Completion

Specify the location of the deployment type's content and other settings that control how content is delivered to target devices. All the contents in the path specified will be delivered.

Content location: `\\sccmsrv-01\PackageSource\Java\UninstalScrip`   [Browse...]

☐ Persist content in the client cache

☑ Allow clients to share content with other clients on the same subnet

This option allows clients that use Windows BranchCache to download content from on-premises distribution points. Content downloads from cloud-based distribution points can always be shared by clients that use Windows BranchCache.

Specify the command used to install this content.

Installation program: `powershell.exe -ExecutionPolicy Bypass -File .\Inv`   [Browse...]

Installation start in:

Configuration Manager can remove installations of this content if an uninstall program is specified below.

Uninstall program: [Browse...]

Uninstall start in:

☐ Run installation and uninstall program as 32-bit process on 64-bit clients.

Click Next.

For the **Detection Method**, choose '**Use a custom script**…' and click **Edit**…

Choose the Script type **PowerShell**, and from the source files, paste the content of the script **Java_Uninstall_Detection_Script.ps1**.

The first line of the script (highlighted in yellow) must contain the **version number** of the version of Java you are deploying. **When updating to a new Java version, this version number in the detection script must also be updated, otherwise the detection will not work. The PowerShell script used in the Update Java section of this guide will do this automatically.**

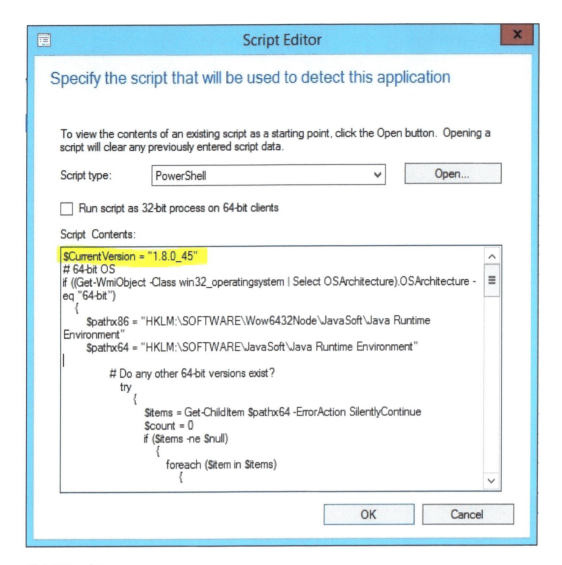

Click OK and Next.

On the **User Experience** page, choose **Install for system**, **Whether or not a user is logged on**, and set the **maximum** and **estimated** times:

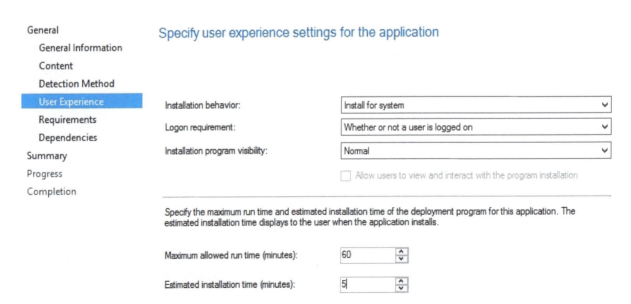

Click Next through the rest of the wizard, and Close to finish.

Create a Dependency

Now right-click the Java **install** deployment type, eg "Java 8 Update 45", and choose **Properties**. On the **Dependencies** tab, click **Add**.

Enter the Dependency group name **Uninstall Java**, then click **Add.** Browse to the Java application you created, and select the **Uninstall Java** deployment type.

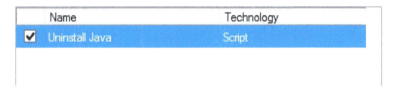

Click OK, and OK again to close the Window

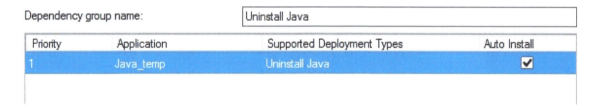

You will now see the dependency in the Application.

Distribute Content

Right-click the Application and choose Distribute Content. Complete the wizard to distribute the content to your distribution points.

Deploy the Application

Once the content distribution has finished, you are ready to deploy the Application.

Before deploying, however, determine if there are any computers in your environment that need to be **excluded** from the deployment, for example because they need to keep a specific older version of Java for application compatibility. These machines should be the exception and not the rule. Create a new **Device Collection** for such computers and add them to it.

Now choose or create a **Device Collection** containing the computers you want to target the deployment to. Right-click the collection, and on the **Membership Rules** tab, add an **Exclude Collections rule**, and choose the collection you created earlier for the excluded computers. This will ensure that those excluded computers do not receive the general Java deployment.

Now right-click the Java Application and choose **Deploy**.

In the **Deploy Software Wizard**, browse to choose the target collection and click Next.

Software:	Java	Browse...
Collection:	All SCCM 2012 Clients	Browse...

☐ Use default distribution point groups associated to this collection

☑ Automatically distribute content for dependencies

Click Next again for the **Content** section.

In the **Deployment Settings** section, choose **Action: Install**, and **Purpose: Required**.

Action:	Install ⌄
Purpose:	Required ⌄

☐ Pre-deploy software to the user's primary device

☐ Send wake-up packets

☐ Allow clients on a metered Internet connection to download content after the installation deadline, which might incur additional costs

Click Next, and set your desired **Deployment Schedule**:

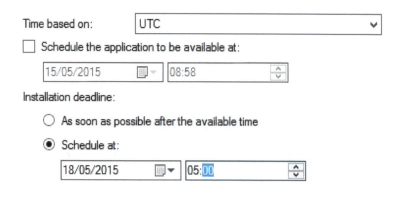

Click Next, and set your desired **User Experience**:

Specify user experience setting for this deployment

User notifications: [Display in Software Center, and only show notifications for computer restarts ˅]

When the installation deadline is reached, allow the following activities to be performed outside the maintenance window:

    ☑ Software Installation

    ☐ System restart (if required to complete the installation)

Write filter handling for Windows Embedded devices

    ☑ Commit changes at deadline or during a maintenance window (requires restarts)

       If this option is not selected, content will be applied on the overlay and committed later.

Click Next, and set the **Alert thresholds** if desired.

Click Next, Next and Close to finish the wizard.

Create a 64-bit Java Application

This section is for those who also want to deploy the 64-bit version of the Java Runtime.

For this application, we will use a more simplified PowerShell script to 'prepare' the machine for the installation, which will kill any running Java processes and any running browsers that may cause the installation to fail. The UNINSTALL script used for the 32-bit Java deployment will also take care of any unwanted versions of 64-bit Java, so as long as the 32-bit Java version is deployed, there is no need for an additional UNINSTALL script.

We can also therefore use a more simplified detection method, which only needs to detect if the current version of 64-bit Java is already installed, and if it isn't, detect whether any browsers or Java applications are currently running.

Create this application using the same procedure as for the 32-bit Java application, but with a few differences, which are detailed below.

Application Settings

1. Download and use the **64-bit** Java binary
2. Name the Application **Java (x64)**
3. On the **General** section of the **Create Application Wizard**, do **not** select the option **'Run installation and uninstall program as 32-bit process on 64-bit client'**

Create a PREPARE Deployment Type

Instead of creating the additional UNINSTALL deployment type, create a deployment type called **Prepare for Java x64 Install.** Make this a **dependency** of the INSTALL deployment type in the same way as described for the 32-bit Java application.

From the source files, copy the PowerShell script **Stop-JavaProcessesAndBrowsers.ps1** to a subfolder in your Package source, for example \\<Sccmserver>\PackageSource\Java\Preparex64Java. Use this script as the content for the deployment type.

For the **detection method**, use the script **Javax64_Preparation_Detection_Script.ps1** from the source files. This script will check whether the currently deployed version of 64-bit Java is already installed, and if so the **Stop-JavaProcessesAndBrowsers.ps1** does not need to run. If it is **not** installed, the detection script will check for any running browser or Java-related processes, and if found, the **Stop-JavaProcessesAndBrowsers.ps1** script will run to prepare for the 64-bit Java installation.

Create a Global Condition to Detect Operating System Architecture

Because the 64-bit Java will only run on a 64-bit Operating System, we will set a requirement on each deployment type that it must have a 64-bit OS installed. To do that, we will create a custom **Global Condition** that will use WMI to determine the OS architecture of the client machine.

In the ConfigMgr console, navigate to **Software Library > Application Management > Global Conditions**

In the Ribbon, click **Create Global Condition**. Enter the following values:

1. **Name**: OS Architecture
2. **Description**: Checks the architecture of the Operating System
3. **Device type**: Windows
4. **Condition type**: Setting
5. **Setting type**: WQL Query
6. **Data type**: String
7. **Namespace**: root\cimv2
8. **Class**: Win32_OperatingSystem
9. **Property**: OSArchitecture

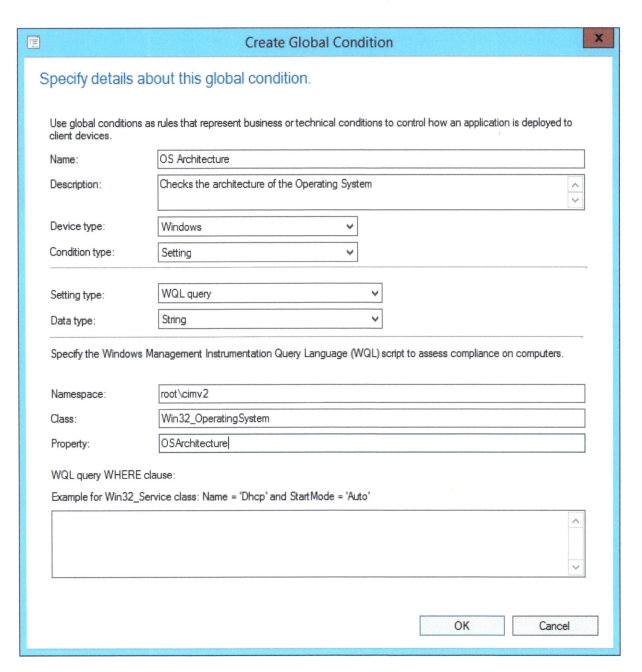

Click OK to save the Global Condition.

Add a 64-bit OS Requirement to Each Deployment Type

For **each deployment type** in the Application, set the requirement for 64-bit OS.

Right-click the deployment type and choose **Properties**. On the **Requirements** tab, click **Add**. Set the following values:

1. **Category**: Custom
2. **Condition**: OS Architecture
3. **Rule type**: Value
4. **Operator**: Equals
5. **Value**: 64-bit

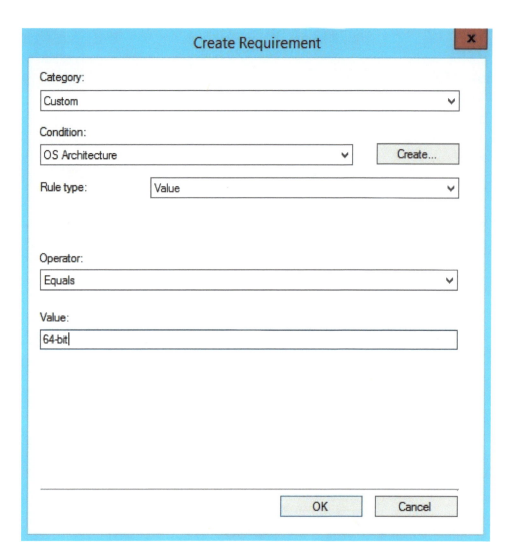

Click OK and save and close the deployment type properties window.

Control Java

In addition to deploying Java, we also want to control how Java is configured on our client machines. To do this, we will deploy a system-wide **deployment.properties** file, where we can set the configuration of Java for all users of the computer.

To ensure that this configuration remains in place, we will use Configuration Manager's **Compliance Settings**, which will allow us both to deploy these settings and to ensure that they are not changed, by remediating any machines that fall out of compliance.

In all, we will create four compliance settings:

1. **Java Deployment Files** – deploys two files, deployment.config and deployment.properties, to the local machine.
2. **Deployment.config Content** – sets the content of the deployment.config file, which defines the location of the system-level deployment.properties file on the client. Once deployed, this setting does not need to change.
3. **Deployment.properties Content** – sets the content of the deployment.properties file which sets the configuration of Java on the client. Once deployed, this setting could be changed to control the content of the file, for example to add an additional setting in the Java configuration.
4. **Java AutoUpdate** – sets the JavaAutoupdate policy directly in the registry

The deployment.properties file can be used to set and / or lock the configuration of the Java Control Panel, and contains many settings that are documented on the Oracle website:

http://docs.oracle.com/javase/8/docs/technotes/guides/deploy/properties.html

In this demonstration, we will set the Java Web Start autodownload feature to never automatically download and then lock it, which will remove the **Update** tab in the Java Control panel.

It is also possible to use Compliance settings in ConfigMgr to create and manage an "exception.sites" file, which can be used to define which sites can bypass some of the common security checks that Java runs. This is the "Exception site list" found on the Security tab in the Java Control Panel. In practice however, this may not be the best solution, as it would lock that setting and prevent users from adding any additional sites in their local Java installation – all sites in the exception list would need to be added for all users / computers to whom the Compliance setting is deployed, which could create undesired administration overhead, and a potential security concern (why allow a site if it isn't needed by everyone?)

The exception site list can also be managed using the **Java Deployment Ruleset**, but this is beyond the scope of this guide.

Create a Configuration Item

In this section we will create a Configuration Item that contains the four Compliance settings above.

Create the Configuration Item

In the ConfigMgr Console, navigate to **Assets and Compliance > Compliance Settings > Configuration Items**. In the ribbon, click **Create Configuration Item**.

1. **Name**: Java Configuration
2. **Description**: Configuration settings for Java Control Panel

Configuration items define a configuration and associated validation criteria to be assessed for compliance on client devices.

Name: Java Configuration

Description: Configuration settings for Java Control Panel

Specify the type of configuration item that you want to create:

Windows

☐ This configuration item contains application settings

Assigned categories to improve searching and filtering:

Categories...

Click Next, and on the **Supported Platforms** page, deselect any not-applicable Windows versions.

Create the "Java Deployment Files" Compliance Setting

This Compliance Setting will check the path "$env:windir\Sun\Java\Deployment" on the client machine for the existence of both the **deployment.config** file and the **deployment.properties** file. If they do not exist, they will be created by the remediation script. The **deployment.config** file **MUST** be located in this directory, and for convenience we will locate both files there.

Still in the **Create Configuration Item Wizard**, on the **Settings** page, click **New**.

On the **General** tab, enter the following values:

1. **Name**: Java Deployment Files
2. **Description**: Deploys the deployment.config and the deployment.properties files and sets the initial content
3. **Setting** type: Script
4. **Data** type: String

Discovery Script

In the **Discovery script** section, click **Add Script...**

Choose the **Script language** of Windows PowerShell and paste the content of the **Compliance_Java_Deployment_Files_Discovery.ps1** script from the source files. Click OK to close.

Remediation Script

In the **Remediation script** section, click **Add Script...**

Choose the **Script language** of Windows PowerShell and paste the content of the **Compliance_Java_Deployment_Files_Remediation.ps1** script from the source files. Click OK to close.

The remediation script will set the content of the deployment.config file to the following. The mandatory setting means the system-level deployment.properties file **must** be used.

```
deployment.system.config=file:///C:/Windows/Sun/Java/Deployment/deployment.properti
es
deployment.system.config.mandatory=true
```

The remediation script will set the content of the deployment.properties file to the following, and you can add your own customizations:

```
deployment.javaws.autodownload=NEVER
deployment.javaws.autodownload.locked
deployment.expiration.check.enabled=FALSE
```

Create a Compliance Rule

Here we will create a rule that defines the criteria for compliance to the configuration setting. If the output of the discovery script returns '**Compliant**', then the criteria is met, the computer is compliant to the setting and no further action is needed. If the discovery script returns any other value, the computer is not compliant, and the remediation script will run to correct the non-compliance.

On the Compliance Rules tab of the Compliance Setting, click New. Enter the following values and click OK to save:

1. **Name**: Compliant
2. **The value returned by the specified script**: Equals
3. **The following values**: Compliant
4. **Run the specified remediation script when this setting is noncompliant**
5. **Noncompliance severity for reports**: Warning

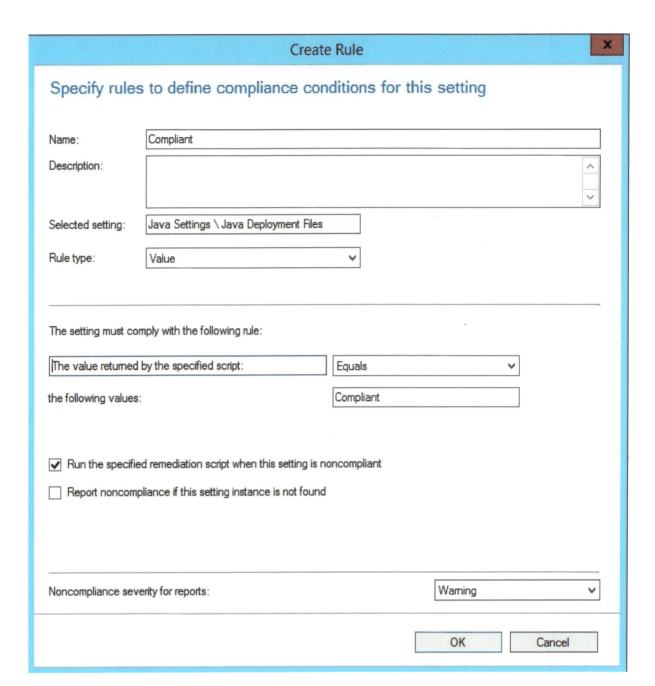

Click OK to save and close the Compliance setting.

Create the "Deployment.config Content" Compliance Setting

This Compliance setting will check the content of the **deployment.config** file against the value defined in the discovery script. If the file has been changed in any way and no longer matches the defined value, the remediation script will run and set the file content back to what it should be.

This setting ensure that the content of the file is not changed, and can also be used to update the content of the file on all targeted machines by changing the defined value in **both** the discovery and remediation scripts.

Create a new **Compliance setting** and **rule** using the same process as before, but using the following scripts from the source files for discovery and remediation:

Discovery Script: **Compliance_deployment_config_Discovery.ps1**

Remediation Script: **Compliance_deployment_config_Remediation.ps1**

Create the "Deployment.properties Content" Compliance Setting

This Compliance setting will check the content of the **deployment.properties** file against the value defined in the discovery script. If the file has been changed in any way and no longer matches the defined value, the remediation script will run and set the file content back to what it should be.

This setting ensure that the content of the file is not changed, and can also be used to update the content of the file on all targeted machines by changing the defined value in **both** the discovery and remediation scripts.

Create a new **Compliance setting** and **rule** using the same process as before, but using the following scripts from the source files for discovery and remediation:

Discovery Script: **Compliance_deployment_properties_Discovery.ps1**

Remediation Script: **Compliance_deployment_properties_Remediation.ps1**

Create the "Java AutoUpdate" Compliance Setting

This Compliance setting will be used to also disable and lock the Java AutoUpdate feature by setting the registry keys directly. The policy is set in the following registry branch and keys:

HKLM:\SOFTWARE\JavaSoft\Java Update\Policy
HKLM:\SOFTWARE\Wow6432Node\Javasoft\Java Update\Policy

1. EnableAutoUpdateCheck
2. EnableJavaUpdate
3. NotifyDownload
4. NotifyInstall

Create a new **Compliance setting** and **rule** using the same process as before, but using the following scripts from the source files for discovery and remediation:

Discovery Script: **Compliance_deployment_properties_Discovery.ps1**

Remediation Script: **Compliance_deployment_properties_Remediation.ps1**

Finish Up

Now you should have the four settings and the four compliance rules in the Configuration Item. Click next through the rest of the **Create Configuration Item Wizard** to finish.

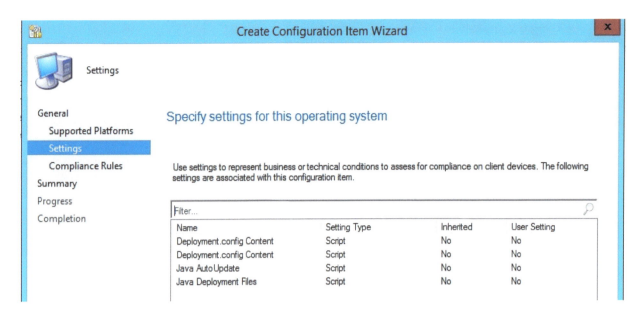

Create a Configuration Baseline

Create

Now we will create a new **Configuration Baseline** that will be used to deploy the Configuration Item and its settings to our client machines.

In the ConfigMgr Console, click on **Configuration Baselines**, and click **Create Configuration Baseline** in the ribbon.

Name it **Java Configuration**, then in the **Configuration data** section, click **Add > Configuration Items**. Select the Configuration Item you created and click **Add**, then OK. Click OK again to save the baseline.

Deploy

Right-click the Configuration Baseline and choose **Deploy**. Check the options to **Remediate noncompliant rules when supported**, and **Allow remediation outside the maintenance window**. Choose your target **collection** and set the **schedule**. Click OK to save and finish.

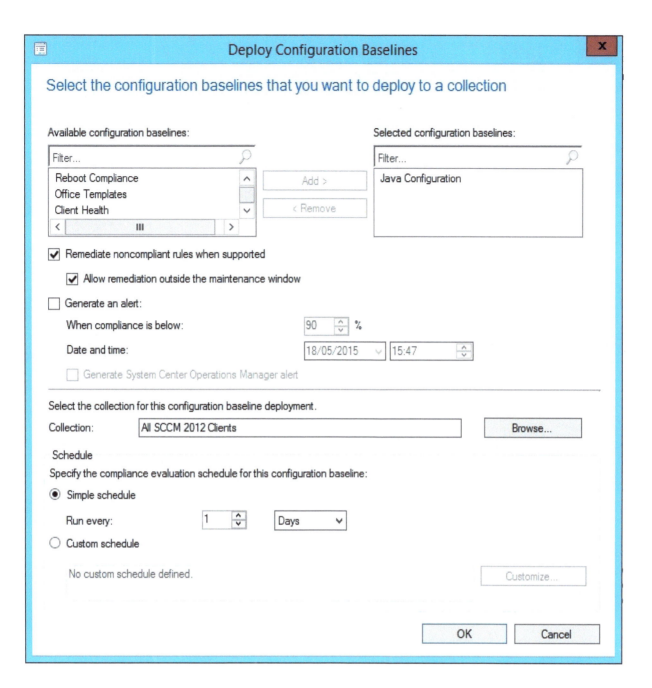

Deploy Configuration Baselines

Select the configuration baselines that you want to deploy to a collection

Available configuration baselines:

Filter...

Reboot Compliance
Office Templates
Client Health

Selected configuration baselines:

Filter...

Java Configuration

Add >

< Remove

☑ Remediate noncompliant rules when supported

☑ Allow remediation outside the maintenance window

☐ Generate an alert:

When compliance is below: 90   %

Date and time: 18/05/2015   15:47

☐ Generate System Center Operations Manager alert

Select the collection for this configuration baseline deployment.

Collection: All SCCM 2012 Clients   Browse...

Schedule

Specify the compliance evaluation schedule for this configuration baseline:

◉ Simple schedule

Run every: 1   Days

○ Custom schedule

No custom schedule defined.   Customize...

OK   Cancel

27 Control Java

Update Java

Now that we have deployed Java to our machines and set the configuration using Compliance settings, we will need to periodically update the Java version on our clients. To do this manually requires the following steps:

1. Download and extract the new Java binaries
2. Copy to the ConfigMgr Package source
3. Set the deployment deadline of the Java application into the future to prevent any clients from running it while it is being updated
4. Delete or disable the old INSTALL deployment type in the Java application
5. Create a new INSTALL deployment type the Java application
6. Add the dependency of the UNINSTALL DT (or the PREPARE DT for the 64-bit Java) to the new INSTALL DT
7. On the 64-bit application only, set the requirement for 64-bit OS on the new iNSTALL deployment type
8. Update the Java version code in the UNINSTALL (or PREPARE) DT detection method script
9. Wait for content distribution to complete
10. Change the deployment deadline to a new start date

After the next Machine Policy Retrieval and Evaluation Cycle, our client machines that have already been targeted with the previous deployment of Java will then detect that the Java application has been updated and is no longer installed because of the new MSI code in the new deployment type, and will proceed to uninstall the current version and install the new one based on the settings of your deployment.

If you want to test the deployment of the new version on a few selected machines before deploying to *all* your client machines, you can simply disable or remove the current application deployment, and create a new deployment to the collection that contains your test machines. I prefer simply to set the deadline of the deployment into the distant future so it will not run, then when I'm done testing and ready to deploy it globally, I simply change the deadline back to the new start date.

This update process is easy enough to do manually, but it can be made even easier by automating with PowerShell. In the source files is a script that will do these update activities for you. You simply enter the application name, the targeted collection name from the deployment, and the new deadline date and time as parameters. It will then perform the following activities:

1. Renames the existing INSTALL deployment type with a prefix of "Old_".
2. Sets a dummy requirement rule on the existing INSTALL deployment type of "Total Physical memory less than 9MB" to effectively disable it. Just in case something were to go wrong with the new deployment, we keep the old deployment type in place but disabled until we are ready to delete it.
3. Set the deadline of the existing deployment into the distant future, effectively disabling it and preventing any installations while we update the application
4. Download, extract and copy the new Java binary to the SCCM package source if they are not already present
5. Create a new INSTALL deployment type from the new Java MSI
6. Add the UNINSTALL (or PREPARE for 64-bit) deployment type as a dependency for the new INSTALL deployment type

7. For 64-bit only, set the 64-bit OS requirement on the new INSTALL deployment type
8. Update the detection method script with the version code of the new Java version
9. Re-order the deployment type priorities so the INSTALL deployment type has the highest priority and evaluates first
10. Set a new deadline for the deployment

Update Java with PowerShell

From the source files, copy the script **New-JavaDeployment.ps1** to your ConfigMgr site server. The script uses a combination of methods including cmdlets from the Configuration Manager PowerShell module, WMI and the .Net Framework. It must be run as administrator and have internet access (no proxy is specified).

Note: the script will only work as intended if the applications and deployment types were created as described in this guide.

Non-Mandatory Parameters

The script has 2 non-mandatory parameters that are a good idea to set in the script before you run it, as these parameters may not change. They can be found in the parameter section of the script after the comment based help.

JavaPackageSourceLocal
The local path on the server to the directory where your Java source files will be stored, eg
G:\PackageSource\Java

JavaPackageSourceRemote
The remote UNC path to the same directory where your Java source files will be stored, eg
\\sccmsrv-01\PackageSource\Java

Examples

Update the 32-bit Java Application
The following command will create a new deployment type of the latest 32-bit Java release for the application "Java". The deadline of the deployment targeted to the "All SCCM 2012 Clients" collection will be updated to the new date and time specified. The default PackageSource locations defined in the script will be used.

```
.\New-JavaDeployment.ps1 -ApplicationName "Java" -TargetedCollection
"All SCCM 2012 Clients" -DeployDeadlineDate 22/06/2016 -
DeployDeadlineTime 15:00
```

Update the 64-bit Java Application
The following command will create a new deployment type of the latest 64-bit Java release for the application "Java (x64)". The deadline of the deployment targeted to the "All SCCM 2012 Clients" collection will be updated to the new date and time specified. The default PackageSource locations defined in the script will be used.

```
$params = @{
    x64 = $True
    ApplicationName = "Java (x64)"
    TargetedCollection = "All SCCM 2012 Clients"
    DeployDeadlineDate = "22/06/2016"
```

```
DeployDeadlineTime = "15:00"
}
.\New-JavaDeployment.ps1 @params
```

Output

The script will return output to the console similar to below. Note that when the Java binary is downloaded, the script will execute it just long enough for the MSI to be extracted, then it will kill the executable. You may see a Java installation window appear briefly, but it will disappear within a couple of seconds.

```
#######################
# New Java Deployment #
#######################

Action: Disabling old deployment type with dummy requirement
Action: Renaming old Java deployment type
Action: Setting the deployment deadline into the distant future
Action: Finding latest Java version
Action: Downloading jre-8u45-windows-x64.exe
Info: Download completed in 0 minutes and 12 seconds
Action: Extracting files
Please IGNORE the Java installation window if it appears!
Action: Copying extracted files to packagesource
Action: Creating new deployment type
Action: Updating new deployment type
Action: Performing additional deployment type updates
Action: Re-ordering deployment type priorities
Action: Setting new deployment deadline
```

Reporting on Your Java Deployments

Use the Built-in Tools

There are a few ways you can monitor the status of your Java Application deployments, for example you can use the built-in SSRS reporting where the "**Application compliance**" report can give you basic information.

Application compliance
⊞ Description

Application	Success	Requirements Not Met	Error	Total	
Java	38	0	0		38

You can also use the ConfigMgr console. For example, click on the **Deployments** tab for the Application, and you will see a **Compliance** figure as a percentage for each deployment. You can also add additional columns to the view, such as **Number Success, Number Errors, Number In Progress** etc.

Java

Icon	Collection	Deployment Start Time	Compliance %	Assets Targeted	Deadline	Number Errors	Number In Progress	Number Success
	Rollout: Java 32-bit Global	01/07/2018 03:00	0.0		01/01/2099 23:10			
	All Information Systems Computers for Java	22/05/2015 03:00	88.4	43	22/05/2015 03:00	0	4	38
	Java	17/10/2014 14:36	0.0	0	17/10/2015 15:00	0	0	0

The most amount of detail can be found from **Monitoring Node > Deployments**. Click on your deployment and you can see summary statistics. However, the way ConfigMgr summarizes data can be misleading, as can be seen both in the SSRS report, the Application Deployment summary, and here in the **Completion Statistics**. For example, here it tells me I have 38 machines in the '**Success**' status, 4 'In **Progress**' and 1 '**Unknown**'. 38+4+1 = 43, which is the correct number of client machines in the targeted collection, however this application has been deployed to machines in different global time-zones, and some of them have not yet reached the deadline to run this application and therefore would have reported no results. Therefore these summary statistics are not quite true.

To find out why, we need to go directly to the SQL database. If I run the following SQL query using the AssignmentID of the deployment, I discover that some results are being returned for *older* revisions of the application where there are no results for the *current* revision. This data would actually represent a *previous* deployment, and these old results are being included in the summary data. The information returned at this level is therefore unfortunately not always accurate.

SQL Query:

```sql
SELECT TargetCollectionID,
       AssignmentID,
       app.ResourceID,
       Descript,
       ComplianceState,
       EnforcementState,
       Revision,
       sys.Name0
FROM dbo.vAppDeploymentResultsPerClient app
inner join dbo.v_R_System sys on app.ResourceID = sys.resourceID
where AssignmentID = '16777542'
order by sys.name0
```

SQL Query Results:

	TargetCollectionID	AssignmentID	ResourceID	Descript	ComplianceState	EnforcementState	Revision	Name0
1	0019B	16777542	16778385	Java	1	1000	55	
2	0019B	16777542	16777400	Java	1	1000	49	
3	0019B	16777542	16778835	Java	1	1000	55	
4	0019B	16777542	16780524	Java	NULL	4000	NULL	
5	0019B	16777542	16777966	Java	1	1000	55	
6	0019B	16777542	16778845	Java	1	1000	44	
7	0019B	16777542	16777967	Java	1	1000	55	
8	0019B	16777542	16777401	Java	6	2009	49	
9	0019B	16777542	16778879	Java	1	1000	55	
10	0019B	16777542	16779713	Java	1	1000	44	

The good thing is you can get more accurate information by clicking the **View Status** link in the Completion Statistics, where you can see individual results categorized by the deployment status. This view can be useful for troubleshooting, as for any machines that failed you can find an error code and description.

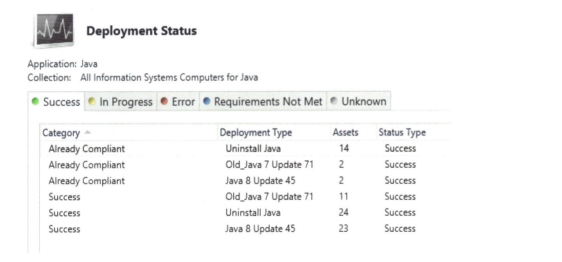

Deployment Status

Application: Java
Collection: All Information Systems Computers for Java

● Success   ● In Progress   ● Error   ● Requirements Not Met   ● Unknown

Category ▲	Deployment Type	Assets	Status Type
Already Compliant	Uninstall Java	14	Success
Already Compliant	Old_Java 7 Update 71	2	Success
Already Compliant	Java 8 Update 45	2	Success
Success	Old_Java 7 Update 71	11	Success
Success	Uninstall Java	24	Success
Success	Java 8 Update 45	23	Success

Asset Details

Filter

Device ▲	User	Error Code	Error Description	Description
	(SYSTEM)	0x87D00314 (-2016410860)	CI Version Info timed out.	

In the Deployments Node, you can also click on the **Deployment Types** tab for the deployment, where a nice graphical summary is displayed for each deployment type:

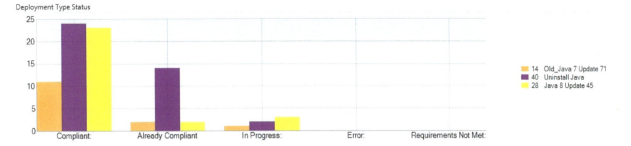

Java Status to All Information Systems Computers for Java

Create a Custom Deployment Report with Microsoft Excel

Microsoft Excel is an excellent tool for reporting, and since it can also be used to query a SQL server, we can create dynamic reports that retrieve real-time information from the ConfigMgr database which we can display both in raw and graphical form, in a single report. We can also use Excel's powerful formulas to further summarize the data, and customize exactly how we want to display it.

Included in the source files for this guide is an example deployment report that we will use to report on our Java deployment. Also included are some ODC (Office Data Connection) files that we will add to the report to query the ConfigMgr database.

PreRequisities

You will need to have at least read-only (**db_datareader**) access to your ConfigMgr database with your **logged-on** account as we will use integrated security to access the database, and you will need to know the name of the SQL server and Instance, and the name of the ConfigMgr database.

Find the AssignmentID of the Deployment

In the ConfigMgr console, click on the Java application, and click on the **Deployments** tab at the bottom. Right-click one of the column headers and select **Assignment ID** from the list. The Assignment ID number will now be displayed in table. Make a note of the Assignment ID for the deployment you want to report on; we will add this to the ODC files.

Customize the ODC Files

In the source files are two ODC files:

1. **Java_Deployment_Summary.odc**
2. **Java_Deployment_Data.odc**

The first ODC file will query the summary data for the application deployment and link it with some data about the targeted collection. The second ODC file will query for the enforcement state of the deployment on each client computer targeted.

Edit the **Java_Deployment_Summary** ODC file in Notepad. Search for the line that begins **<odc:ConnectionString>**. In this connection string, update the following values:

Initial Catalog=CM_ABC - the name of your ConfigMgr database

Data Source=sccmsqlsrv\INST_SCCM – your ConfigMgr SQL server and instance

Now search for the line that begins **<odc:CommandText>**. This contains the SQL query that will run. Replace the Assignment ID value with your new value, eg *AssignmentID = '16777542'*

Make the same edits for the **Java_Deployment_Data** ODC file. This Assignment ID can be found at the very end of the SQL query.

Import the Connections into the Excel Report

From the source files, open the **ConfigMgr_Deployment_Report_Template.xlsx**. You will see that the charts display no data.

Click on the **Applications** worksheet. In the ribbon, click **Data > Existing Connections**. In the bottom left of the Existing Connections window, click **Browse for More**. Locate and select the **Java_Deployment_Summary** ODC file.

In the **Import Data** window, ensure that you enter the data as a **Table in the existing worksheet** at cell **A1**, then click **Properties** at the bottom left:

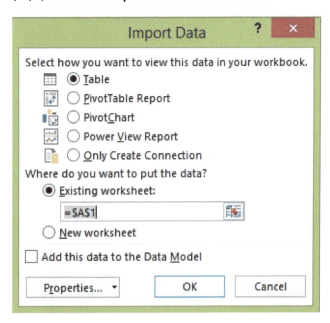

In the **Connection Properties** window, check the box **Refresh data when opening the file** so that the latest data is always retrieved from the database whenever the report is opened.

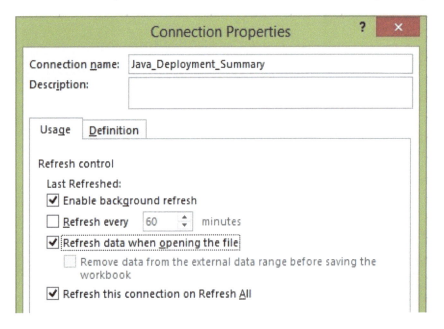

Click OK and OK in the Import Data window to save and close.

You should now see some data entered in the worksheet:

A	B	C	D	E	F	G	H	I	J	K	L	M
CI_ID	ParentID	TargetCollectionID	AssignmentID	Descript	DeploymentTime	ModificationTime	OfferTypeID	AlreadyPresent	Success	InProgress	Unknown	Error	Req
16859400	16859400	▮▮▮▮19B		16777542	Java	22/05/2015 03:00	21/05/2015 12:50	0	0	38	4	1	0

Click on the **Deploy Data** worksheet and do the same as before, this time importing the **Java_Deployment_Data** ODC file. When finished, you will see data returned into the worksheet:

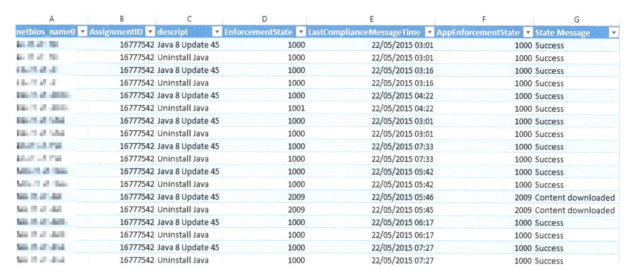

netbios_name0	AssignmentID	descript	EnforcementState	LastComplianceMessageTime	AppEnforcementState	State Message
	16777542	Java 8 Update 45	1000	22/05/2015 03:01	1000	Success
	16777542	Uninstall Java	1000	22/05/2015 03:01	1000	Success
	16777542	Java 8 Update 45	1000	22/05/2015 03:16	1000	Success
	16777542	Uninstall Java	1000	22/05/2015 03:16	1000	Success
	16777542	Java 8 Update 45	1000	22/05/2015 04:22	1000	Success
	16777542	Uninstall Java	1001	22/05/2015 04:22	1000	Success
	16777542	Java 8 Update 45	1000	22/05/2015 03:01	1000	Success
	16777542	Uninstall Java	1000	22/05/2015 03:01	1000	Success
	16777542	Java 8 Update 45	1000	22/05/2015 07:33	1000	Success
	16777542	Uninstall Java	1000	22/05/2015 07:33	1000	Success
	16777542	Java 8 Update 45	1000	22/05/2015 05:42	1000	Success
	16777542	Uninstall Java	1000	22/05/2015 05:42	1000	Success
	16777542	Java 8 Update 45	2009	22/05/2015 05:46	2009	Content downloaded
	16777542	Uninstall Java	2009	22/05/2015 05:45	2009	Content downloaded
	16777542	Java 8 Update 45	1000	22/05/2015 06:17	1000	Success
	16777542	Uninstall Java	1000	22/05/2015 06:17	1000	Success
	16777542	Java 8 Update 45	1000	22/05/2015 07:27	1000	Success
	16777542	Uninstall Java	1000	22/05/2015 07:27	1000	Success

You will notice that in the **descript** column, each active deployment type is listed. You only really want to report on one at a time, and usually the INSTALL deployment type, so use the Excel filter to select only that deployment type for display:

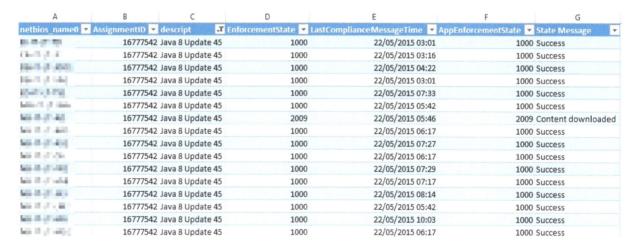

netbios_name0	AssignmentID	descript	EnforcementState	LastComplianceMessageTime	AppEnforcementState	State Message
	16777542	Java 8 Update 45	1000	22/05/2015 03:01	1000	Success
	16777542	Java 8 Update 45	1000	22/05/2015 03:16	1000	Success
	16777542	Java 8 Update 45	1000	22/05/2015 04:22	1000	Success
	16777542	Java 8 Update 45	1000	22/05/2015 03:01	1000	Success
	16777542	Java 8 Update 45	1000	22/05/2015 07:33	1000	Success
	16777542	Java 8 Update 45	1000	22/05/2015 05:42	1000	Success
	16777542	Java 8 Update 45	2009	22/05/2015 05:46	2009	Content downloaded
	16777542	Java 8 Update 45	1000	22/05/2015 06:17	1000	Success
	16777542	Java 8 Update 45	1000	22/05/2015 07:27	1000	Success
	16777542	Java 8 Update 45	1000	22/05/2015 06:17	1000	Success
	16777542	Java 8 Update 45	1000	22/05/2015 07:29	1000	Success
	16777542	Java 8 Update 45	1000	22/05/2015 07:17	1000	Success
	16777542	Java 8 Update 45	1000	22/05/2015 08:14	1000	Success
	16777542	Java 8 Update 45	1000	22/05/2015 05:42	1000	Success
	16777542	Java 8 Update 45	1000	22/05/2015 10:03	1000	Success
	16777542	Java 8 Update 45	1000	22/05/2015 06:17	1000	Success

The rest of the worksheets and charts will now be populated with data.

Understanding the Report

The deployment report contains 6 worksheets / charts as follows:

Deploy Status

This is a column chart that summarizes the deployment status of the application on all the clients targeted.

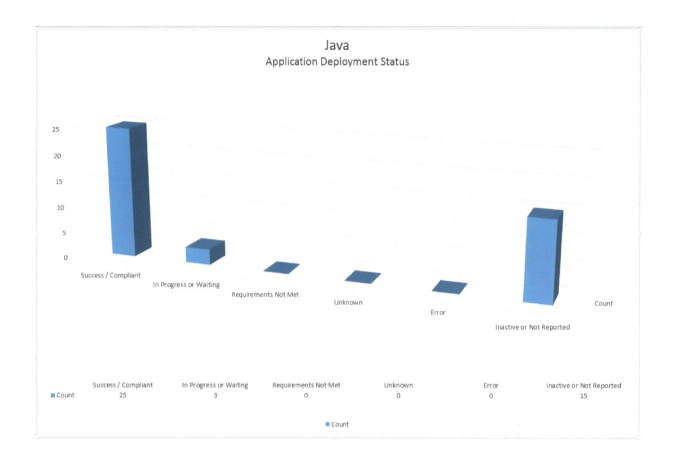

Java
Application Deployment Status

	Success / Compliant	In Progress or Waiting	Requirements Not Met	Unknown	Error	Inactive or Not Reported
Count	25	3	0	0	0	15

■ Count

Deploy Success – Active Only

This is a pie chart that displays the deployment status as a percentage for only those clients that are active and have reported the deployment status to the management point.

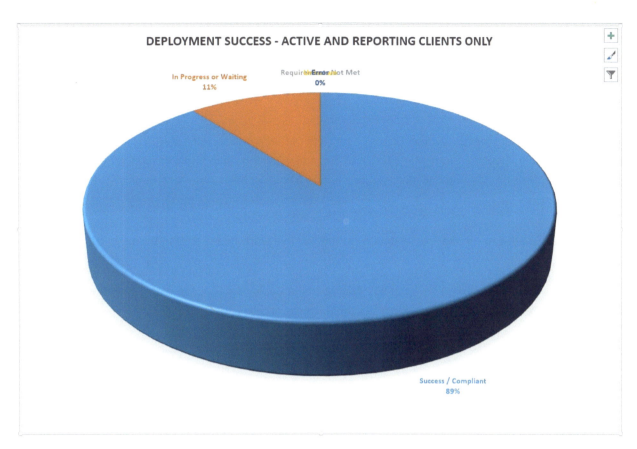

DEPLOYMENT SUCCESS - ACTIVE AND REPORTING CLIENTS ONLY

In Progress or Waiting
11%

Requirements Error Not Met
0%

Success / Compliant
89%

Deploy Success – ALL

This is a pie chart that displays the deployment status as a percentage for all targeted clients.

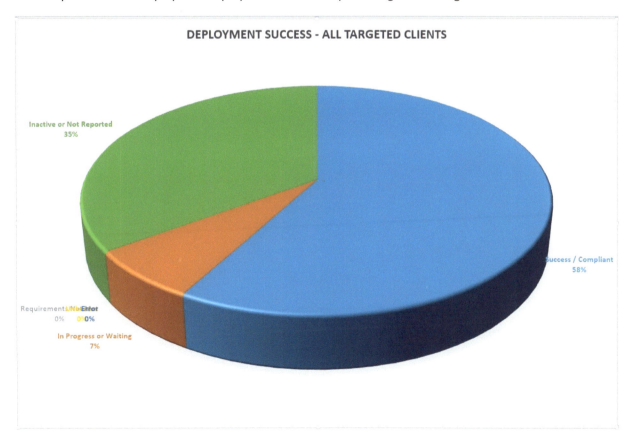

DEPLOYMENT SUCCESS - ALL TARGETED CLIENTS

Inactive or Not Reported
35%

Success / Compliant
58%

Requirement Not Error
0%   0% 0%

In Progress or Waiting
7%

Applications

This worksheet returns summary data for the deployment and the targeted collection from the ConfigMgr database

Deploy Data

This worksheet returns the deployment status of each client that has reported a status to the management point, from the ConfigMgr database. You can use the column filters to filter for a particular state message, for example, and find all computers with a particular error state for troubleshooting.

Summary

This worksheet is used to summarize the data from the last two worksheets, and is the source for the three charts.

By default, it will summarize data for up to 99999 rows in the Deploy Data worksheet, although you can change that number by editing the cell ranges in the formulas in cells B3:B7.

Appendix A

Sample WQL Queries

Included here are some sample WQL queries that can be used to query for Java Runtime installations in your environment. Use them as the query statement in a new query in the Monitoring node of the ConfigMgr Console.

Enable the WMI class in Hardware Inventory

These queries use the **SMS_G_SYSTEM_INSTALLED_SOFTWARE** WMI class, which is not enabled by default and needs to be enabled in the hardware inventory for the clients.

To do so, navigate to **Administration > Client Settings** in the ConfigMgr console. Right-click your client settings and choose **Properties**. Click **Hardware Inventory > Set Classes**.

Scroll down to and put a check against the "**Installed Software – Asset Intelligence (SMS_InstalledSoftware)**" class.

Your clients will start reporting data for this class after their next hardware inventory cycle.

All 32-bit Java Runtime Installations
(filtering out the Java Development Kit and the Java Auto Updater)

select distinct SMS_R_System.Name, SMS_R_System.LastLogonUserName, SMS_G_System_INSTALLED_SOFTWARE.ProductName, SMS_G_System_INSTALLED_SOFTWARE.ProductVersion, SMS_G_System_INSTALLED_SOFTWARE.InstallDate from SMS_R_System inner join SMS_G_System_INSTALLED_SOFTWARE on SMS_G_System_INSTALLED_SOFTWARE.ResourceID = SMS_R_System.ResourceId where SMS_G_System_INSTALLED_SOFTWARE.ProductName like "Java%Update%" and SMS_G_System_INSTALLED_SOFTWARE.ProductName not like "Java%Update%(64-bit)" and SMS_G_System_INSTALLED_SOFTWARE.ProductName not like "%Development%" and SMS_G_System_INSTALLED_SOFTWARE.ProductName not like "%Auto Updater%"

All 64-bit Java Runtime Installations
(filtering out the Java Development Kit and the Java Auto Updater)

select distinct SMS_R_System.Name, SMS_R_System.LastLogonUserName, SMS_G_System_INSTALLED_SOFTWARE.ProductName, SMS_G_System_INSTALLED_SOFTWARE.ProductVersion, SMS_G_System_INSTALLED_SOFTWARE.InstallDate from SMS_R_System inner join SMS_G_System_INSTALLED_SOFTWARE on SMS_G_System_INSTALLED_SOFTWARE.ResourceID = SMS_R_System.ResourceId where SMS_G_System_INSTALLED_SOFTWARE.ProductName like "Java%Update%(64-bit)" and SMS_G_System_INSTALLED_SOFTWARE.ProductName not like

"%Development%" and SMS_G_System_INSTALLED_SOFTWARE.ProductName not like "%Auto Updater%"